MUMMY PORTRAITS

from Roman Egypt

Paul Roberts

MUMMY PORTRAITS

from Roman Egypt

THE BRITISH MUSEUM PRESS

Paul Roberts has asserted the right to be identified
as the author of this work

First published in 2008 by The British Museum Press
A division of The British Museum Company Ltd
38 Russell Square, London WC1B 3QQ
www.britishmuseum.org

A catalogue record for this book is available from
the British Library

ISBN: 978-0-7141-5070-3

Designed and typeset by Martin Richards for
New Leaf Design
Printed in China by C&C Offset Printing

CONTENTS

Introduction 7

Portraits from Hawara 13

Portraits from er-Rubayat 59

Portraits from Other Sites 81

Chronology 94

Further Reading 95

Illustration References 96

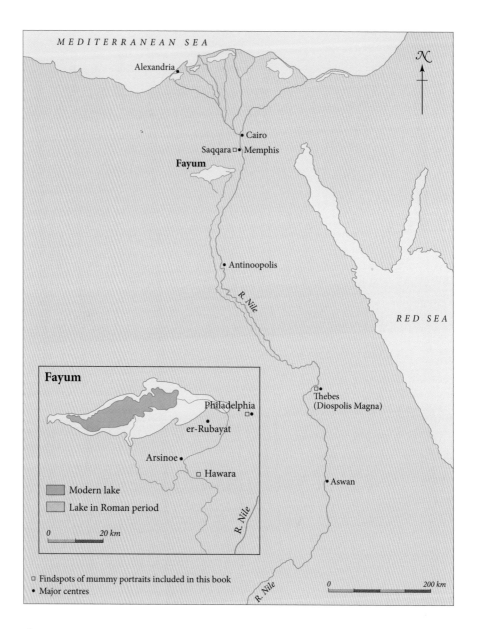

MEDITERRANEAN SEA

Alexandria

Cairo
Saqqara □• Memphis
Fayum

• Antinoopolis

R. Nile

RED SEA

Fayum

Philadelphia
□•
• er-Rubayat

Arsinoe •
□ Hawara

□• Thebes
(Diospolis Magna)

Modern lake

Lake in Roman period

0   20 km

• Aswan

R. Nile

□ Findspots of mummy portraits included in this book
• Major centres

R. Nile

0   200 km

6

INTRODUCTION

I n this book you will meet men, women and children who lived and died in Egypt almost 2000 years ago. Their beautiful, mysterious portraits – many incredibly lifelike – were painted onto thin panels of wood, or covers of canvas or linen, and placed after death on the outer wrappings of their mummies. Together they make up the largest collection of colour images of real people to survive from the ancient world.

These 'mummy portraits' were made between about AD 40 and AD 250, when the Roman empire ruled Egypt. The people depicted were wealthy and powerful and wanted to appear as members of the empire, in Roman realistic style. To this end, they are dressed formally in fine clothes and have Roman hairstyles and jewellery. But the portraits are not just Roman. Importantly, each was originally part of a mummy, one of the most powerful symbols of Egyptian culture and religious beliefs. Furthermore, the names on the portraits, when they are given, are often Greek, underlining the fact that most of the subjects had Greek ancestry. They were the legacy of the army of Alexander the Great, who had conquered Egypt three hundred years before the Romans arrived. Greek by ethnicity, Roman by aspiration and placed in an Egyptian mummy, the people of the portraits truly reflected Egypt's diversity and complex history.

Mummy portraits have been found from the Mediterranean coast of Egypt to the city of Thebes far inland, but the largest concentration of finds comes from the Fayum, a very fertile area surrounding a lake about 100 km south-west of Cairo. The portraits in this book come mostly from two sites in the Fayum – er-Rubayat (Philadelphia) and Hawara (Arsinoe).

No one knew much about these works of art until 1887 when dozens of them were collected in Cairo and displayed in Europe and America by an Austrian collector, Theodor Graf. They were (and are still) often called 'er-Rubayat' portraits because they supposedly originated from the town of that name in the Fayum, but archaeologists now know that they came from the cemetery of Philadelphia in the north of the Fayum. Sadly, nothing is known of their excavation.

A year later, in 1888, Hawara in the south of the Fayum was excavated by Sir William Flinders Petrie, an English Egyptologist. Hawara was the cemetery of the city of Arsinoe, the capital of Greek and Roman Fayum. Today, the cemetery's main feature is the great pyramid of the Pharaoh Amenhemhat III (1840s–1820s BC). But, according to the Greek writer Herodotus, the glory of ancient Hawara was the 'labyrinth', a complex of three thousand rooms which surpassed even the pyramids of Giza. Petrie states clearly that he came to investigate these monuments and the pharaonic tombs that surrounded them.

Petrie excavated at Hawara twice – in 1888 and 1911. Fortunately (and very unusually for that period) he kept careful records of his excavations, including notebooks filled with plans and diagrams and, very importantly for future studies such as this book, full lists of the portraits he found. We also have his excavation journals, which were collated from letters to Hilda Petrie (his wife) and to his financial backers. These give detailed (and dated) accounts of discoveries and of daily life in the camp.

Petrie's primary interest was the pharaonic tombs, but he then announced in his journal: 'The Roman tombs however, may prove the most profitable speculation of all.' He had discovered his first portraits. He immediately recognized their value, both to history, science (and his financial backers). 'These portraits are very rare, ... but lately they have been found at Er Rubaiyat in the Fayum and have been offered at fabulous prices in London and Paris … If we can get two or three a week we shall be well repaid.'

Portraits from the two sites were very different. Most of the Hawara examples were painted in encaustic, in which pigments were mixed with

Hawara, showing the pyramid and one of the simple brick pits where the portrait mummies were found.

melted wax, with a result comparable to oil painting. Petrie comments on 'the very modern style in which the effect is produced', likening them to Constable and Turner. This contrasted with the very different examples from er-Rubayat, which were mostly executed in tempera, with pigments mixed with egg white, producing a watercolour finish. Another difference was the shape. The top of the Hawara portraits were nearly always cut into an arch, sometimes very roughly. This suggests they were reused on the mummy, but had originally served as normal domestic portraits.

The mummies were discovered not in elaborate sarcophagi but buried loosely in simple pits or brick cists in the sand. They were 'huddled away ... irregularly into any sort of hole ... lumped together'. It was a miracle that any portraits had survived at all, considering that they were 'on panels as thin as a sheet of veneer and ... buried in the ground without any protection, the dust lying loose on the painting or on a cloth over it'.

Petrie had a theory about their rough burial: 'No thieves would have taken them out of tombs to rebury them.' Instead, he believed that mummies 'with portraits, were kept above ground ... for years and then finally interred'. They were the 'showpieces of the family ... before being carted off and shoved into this hole'. The mummies had in effect been kept on display, and proof came a century later from excavations in the north of Egypt at el-Alamein. Here the excavators found mortuary temples, built for the worship of ancestors. In subterranean chambers were portrait mummies, stowed away prior to being dumped, just like ones from Hawara. Petrie had been right.

But at what stage of life (or death) were they painted? It has been argued that they were produced after death, but other people believe that they are copies of paintings made earlier in the subject's life. Roman writers tell of funerals featuring portraits of the deceased at different ages.

Either way, Petrie had strong opinions about the people featured in the portraits. He identified his second find as 'a young married woman about 25 of a sweet but dignified expression with beautiful features and a fine complexion.' Another woman was 'very modern in appearance – such as one might meet in any drawing room nowadays', and she was also (with one eye on his backers) 'what auctioneers call highly desirable'. His most memorable description is for a portrait that sadly we have not yet been able to identify, a young man who was 'no beauty certainly ... he looks as if he would have made a very conscientious hardworking curate with a tendency to pulpit hysterics'.

Owing to the circumstances of their burial, many of the portraits were in very bad condition and Petrie (reluctantly) acted as an impromptu conservator. Originally, he advocated treating the portraits 'just like any other old pictures; carefully cleaned and then varnished'. Later, he developed a process whereby he remelted their wax surface with a candle, carefully adding a layer of new wax on the top to seal it. 'I gently washed a bit of one to remove all dirt and then warmed it up. It came out brilliantly fresh ... This will be better than trusting the paintings to the most skilful picture cleaner to clean and varnish.' But the process was not without its problems: 'Any overheating ... blisters and frizzles the paint. Overheating ... makes the old wax dissolve in the sea of new and run everywhere. So it is a risky business.' It is easy to criticize his methods today, but as he himself admitted he was not a trained conservator. Many portraits were certainly so fragile that without Petrie's first aid their surface would not have survived.

Petrie cared about the portraits and looked after them as well as he could. The journals reveal a similar concern for his diggers, too. He treated inflamed eyes, toothache and even a serious haemorrhage with 'very well boiled rice and coffee without any sugar'. Petrie himself was often unwell, suffering from colds, sore eyes caused by sand (and mummy dust!), and from general exhaustion caused by running the excavation.

Petrie liked to keep the portraits together with their mummies because of their greater value for archaeology (and his financial backers), but many were too damaged or rotten. In these cases Petrie removed and carefully labelled the skull, leaving the area near his tent 'so strewn with headless mummies ... that I can hardly get in and out'. Petrie built a hut for the skulls, which he darkly called the 'skullery'.

He was very interested in current scientific theories on the ability to use the skull to investigate racial, social and behavioural characteristics. Petrie sent dozens of them to scientists in England and Germany, but they were all feared lost until 1996 when twenty-five of them surfaced in London. Petrie's identification letters and numbers, matching the portraits, were clearly written on the the side of each skull. Two of these specimens were selected for facial reconstruction at the University Museum of Manchester. For the first time in two thousand years we could gaze at the people behind the portraits.

And this was what they had always hoped for – to be seen, thought about and, most of all, remembered as real people. By gazing at them, you too are helping to fulfil their aim. Some are so realistic that when you look at them you recognize them as someone familar to you: a neighbour, a relative, a friend, even a film star. In antiquity they might have hoped for the respect of a few generations; now the intense interest in the portraits has ensured that these men, women and children will be truly immortal.

PORTRAITS FROM HAWARA

MUMMY OF A CHILD
Hawara, AD 40–55

The canvas portrait of this young boy is still fastened into the bandages of his original mummy, reminding us of the original context of all the portraits that we will see in this book. Canvas portraits are some of the earliest to appear and date to the AD 40s or 50s. The boy's brown hair, fringed but long at the back, frames his face with its extremely large eyes. The shroud is covered with scenes of the funerary rituals of Egyptian religion, and shows the boy with Egyptian deities such as Osiris and Isis. Petrie describes how the boy's mummy was found in early March 1888, 'in a hole' with 'two little girls quite too splendaciously got-up' and a woman. This was probably a family group of mother and two children. With them was 'a woman with painted portrait on canvas'. It is likely that the canvas woman was his mother, now far away in the Archaeological Museum in Cairo, Egypt.

PORTRAIT OF A GIRL
Hawara, *c.* AD 50–70

Petrie records in his journals that the mummies were not found in beautiful tombs. Instead they were discovered in simple pits, often with earth, sand and rocks piled on top of them. Some portraits were smashed, scratched or badly worn, and this young woman is one example. Her portrait has lost a lot of the background, where the paint has flaked away. Those areas that stand out, in particular her red lips, are likely to have been retouched after the portrait was rediscovered. She wears a crescent pendant, a type of jewellery that was fashionable throughout the Roman empire at this time. Her hair is fairly short at the front, falling in locks down her neck and onto her shoulders. Around her head is a gilded wreath, not a common feature on the portraits, which perhaps indicates a person (or family) of particular status. She died in about AD 50–70 and was probably found at Hawara, although she does not appear in Petrie's accounts. She looks at us enigmatically – unrecorded and anonymous.

PORTRAIT OF A WOMAN
Hawara, AD 50–70

This woman's portrait was painted on a linen shroud that had been wrapped around the mummy. When Petrie discovered it, the mummy was badly damaged, but fortunately he was able to save most of the portrait.

The woman is rosy-cheeked with a small rouged mouth. She has beautifully dressed hair, with a gilded central parting and banks of tight curls framing her face. Long ringlets fall either side of her neck, and behind her left shoulder is a large gather of hair, tied with a gold band. A red headband runs across the top of her head, a fashion which seems to have been popular in the AD 50s–70s when Nero ruled the empire.

Unlike many of the portraits painted on wooden panels, this linen example extends down to the subject's arms, revealing a dark green, short-sleeved tunic with black shoulder stripes (*clavi*). Unusually, the woman is not wearing a scarf. Her left hand has almost disappeared, but in her right hand she holds a red folded garland. On both her arms she has a large, ornate bracelet in the form of a snake. She also wears gold ball earrings, just like Roman women across the empire at this time, and a heavy gold necklace with an elegant shell pendant.

Her hairstyle and pose look very similar to those seen in some of the panel portraits, so although Petrie referred to her as a 'mediocre portrait of a lady' he was very pleased when he discovered her. He was sure she was the missing link that proved his supposition that 'panel portraits had developed from painted canvas portraits'.

PORTRAIT OF A WOMAN
Hawara, AD 55–70

This image on a wooden panel shows a beautiful young woman with neatly dressed hair, fine robes and gold jewellery. The artist has made very successful play of light and shade, particularly on her mouth, nose and chin. Her hairstyle has tight curls framing her face, with long ringlets falling behind. This dates her to about the time of the emperor Nero, in the AD 60s, as does her fashionable jewellery – a pair of gold ball earrings and a crescent pendant. It is interesting to think that across the empire people were wearing the same clothes, jewellery and hairstyles. The empire really was a common market of people, goods, fashions and ideas, and this lady, although she lived in Egypt, would not have looked out of place in Rome or Athens.

PORTRAIT OF A WOMAN
Hawara, AD 55–70

This is one of the most striking female portraits to have survived from Hawara. The young woman's long, straight nose, strong cheek bones and thick eyebrows, so heavy that they meet across her eyes, combine to create a face that is undeniably handsome, even if not classically beautiful. Her jewellery comprises gold ball earrings and a gold chain with crescent pendant, both typical of the period and seen on other women found at Hawara (see pp. 18 and 20). Her hairstyle, with its masses of tight curls, is also the same as that worn by these women, but without the long tresses at the back.

Her drapery (see overleaf) is carefully painted in shades of purple, a colour that seems to have been very popular in this period. It may also reflect the financial status of her family as purple dyed cloth was often very expensive. She wears the typical dress of wealthy ladies right across the Roman empire. The main garment was a tunic, usually worn loose fitting and short sleeved. On each shoulder there was a stripe (*clavus*), in this case coloured very dark blue or black, and edged with gold, emphasizing her high status. Only one stripe is visible because her left shoulder is covered by a scarf. Robes such as these would have been made of fine wool or linen, but the very wealthy favoured silk, imported from India and even China.

But this woman's story has a rather strange twist. Petrie liked to take away whole mummies from his excavations if at all possible, but when he discoverd this mummy it was so badly rotted that it fell to pieces. He took the portrait, but strangely he also removed the skull. This is because he was fascinated by the theory of phrenology – that you can tell a person's character, physical and mental well-being and racial origins from analysis of the skull. On each skull Petrie wrote the number or letter corresponding to the portrait found with it. Dozens of skulls were taken away from Hawara, but only twenty-five are known to have survived. In 1997 this lady's skull was sent to Manchester University, along with that of the man on p. 28, for a facial reconstruction. The resulting reconstruction was not a photographic likeness – her features were softer and less elongated – but the essence of her character which the painter captured in the portrait was still there.

PORTRAIT OF A YOUNG MAN
Hawara, *c.* AD 70–120

This portrait from the late first or early second century AD shows a man in his early twenties, with a rather distant, sad expression. His hair is an unruly mass of dark curls and his moustache and beard are drawn thin and patchy, which is perhaps an indication of his young age. But there does not seem to be any obvious explanation for the strange depiction of his other facial features. The long nose is well formed, but the eyes are curiously narrow and oddly angled. The mouth is downturned and the highlight applied to only one half of the chin gives it, and thereby the whole face, a lopsided appearance. In fact, the two halves of his face are very irregular. The biggest peculiarity is the distorted shape of the lower face. The left jaw is shown angular and frontal, while the right jaw is shown in perspective, largely hidden because of the three-quarter turn of the head.

Some people have suggested that the painting reflects a genuine medical or genetic disorder. Others have concluded that this is the work of an unskilled painter, incapable of dealing with the art of perspective. Petrie, as forthright as ever, described the portrait as 'a youngish man ... ugly in subject and rather a daub in execution'.

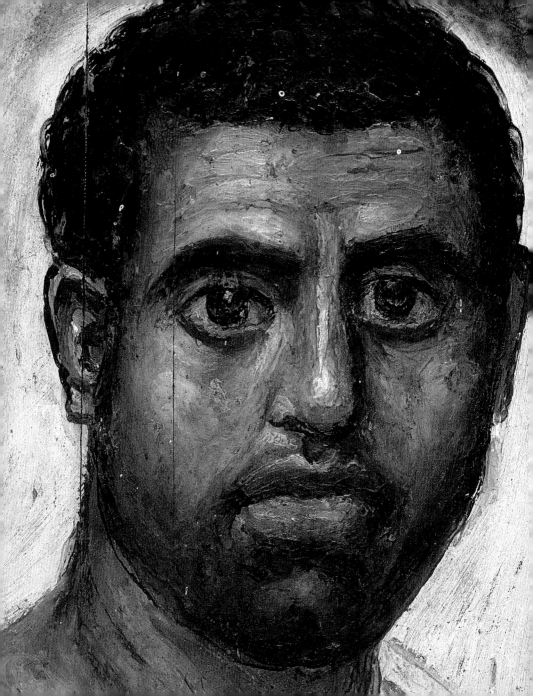

PORTRAIT OF A MAN
Hawara, AD 80–100

This young man, like the subjects of the other portraits from Hawara, was probably a member of the wealthier classes in the city of Arsinoe. Yet he looks as though he would have been more at home in a boxing ring. He is well built and has a very powerful face – a strong brow and nose, a heavy jaw with a growth of stubble and full fleshy lips. His thick dark hair is cut quite short. His face, along with that of a woman (see pp. 22–5), was reconstructed at Manchester University using skulls that Petrie had brought back from Hawara. The process of reconstruction involves making a cast of the skull and then gradually building up over this in clay the relevant muscles, soft tissue and skin, using tissue-thickness data collected from hundreds of human bodies. The reconstruction, made without any reference to the portrait, was cast in bronze-coloured resin. The final head (seen below) is strikingly similar to the portrait and bears features that suggest that he might have had North African or sub-Saharan ancestors. Petrie often commented at length about the portraits, but sadly this was one that he simply labelled 'a middle aged man in good condition'.

PORTRAIT OF A YOUNG MAN
Hawara, *c.* AD 80–120

This young man has undeniably good looks, but a rather vacant stare. With his healthy glow, high cheekbones, strong clean jaw and mass of dark curly hair, he could be found in any Mediterranean city today. His large brown eyes, strong nose and full mouth make his face even more handsome. His faint moustache suggests he may have been in his late teens when he died. Unlike the other portraits seen so far, he is shown naked, and his skin has a definite tanned appearance. This indicates that he may have been an *ephebe*, a Greek word for a young man who took part in the system of physical and cultural training that would equip him for high positions in society and the army. Petrie did not rate this portrait particularly highly, describing it as 'of clear careful hard work without any enterprise ... an early piece by one of the good masters, rather than the ultimatum of a poor hand'.

The mummies were often found heaped one on top of the other; sometimes they were in groups and were possibly members of the same family. This young man had another mummy underneath him. This lower mummy had a painted inscription on his shroud and a wooden label tied to his feet that identified him as Diogenes, a tailor who lived in a suburb of the city of Arsinoe.

PORTRAIT OF A MAN
Hawara, AD 100–120

This is one of the most imposing and authoritative portraits from the cemetery at Hawara. The subject was clearly used to commanding respect, and it is easy to imagine him as a judge or another of the highest officials of the city of Arsinoe. He is probably about forty to fifty years old, though his craggy features make him seem older. He has a heavy brow and heavily lidded brown eyes with thick arched eyebrows, broad cheekbones, a long nose and very pronounced furrows between the mouth and cheeks. He has a very Roman appearance and his *Romanitas* (Roman-ness) is particularly emphasized by his hair, which is combed and cut in a rolled fringe. This style was favoured by the emperor Trajan, who ruled the empire at the beginning of the second century AD. The man shown here looks as though he would have been more at home in Rome than in the Egyptian city of Arsinoe, but perhaps he was typical of many people living there who were Roman, or who wanted to appear as if they were.

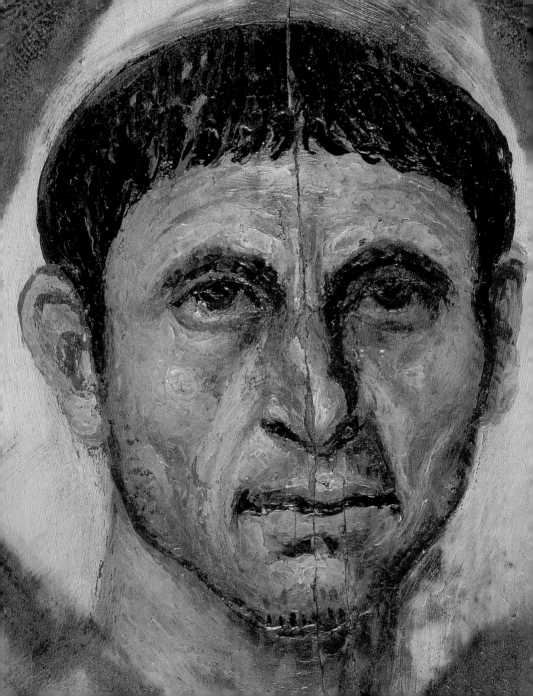

PORTRAIT OF A MAN
Hawara, AD 100–120

This man looks out at us through a small 'window' of original colour. The rest of the portrait is heavily discoloured, indicating the area that was covered with the oiled and resined bandages used during mummification. These were removed when Petrie separated the portrait from its body, something he only did when the bodies were too damaged and rotted to preserve intact.

The subject of this portrait has a lined brow, a short hooked nose and a broad full mouth framed by deep furrows. His hair is combed forward and cut in a short fringe, a style also seen in the previous portrait; it suggests a similar date of the early second century AD. The man's body is shown without clothes, normally an indication that the person was an *ephebe*, in training for civic and military service. These youths are normally portrayed in their teens, but the man in the portrait is clearly older, perhaps in his thirties or forties. Nakedness in the portrait of an older man might suggest nobility or that he was an athlete, even after his teens. Petrie describes how he found, on 8 March 1888, a portrait of 'an old man much like Julius Caesar, awfully scraggy'.

MUMMY OF A YOUNG BOY
Hawara, AD 100–120

This boy in his early teens is still preserved in his original mummy. His large, round staring eyes with their thick arched eyebrows give his gaze a particular intensity. His dark hair is cut in a style dating to the decades around AD 100. Mummification was a lengthy and expensive process, but the relatives of this little boy wanted him to have a suitably grand vehicle to take him to the afterlife. In addition to having a fine portrait, his body was beautifully decorated with diamond patterns, formed by layering six levels of mummy bandages with a small gilded button at the centre of each diamond. He even had a gilded foot case. But inside the mummy all was not well. Scans show that the body is badly disjointed and the skull separated, suggesting either that the persons who mummified the body were less than careful, or that the body was already badly decomposed when it was processed. Unfortunately, when the mummy was discovered in April 1888, Petrie had such a bad cold that he 'could not even look at [this] fine new portrait'.

PAINTED STUCCO MUMMY OF A YOUNG MAN
Hawara, AD 100–120

This well-preserved painted mummy contains the body of a young man called Artemidorus. He was originally mummified in the customary manner, with layers of tight bandaging, but was then covered in plaster, which was in turn brightly painted and gilded.

In many ways Artemidorus represents the melting pot of cultures and influences that typified Roman Egypt and the empire as a whole. His name is Greek and is included in a painted inscription, 'Farewell Artemidorus', written in Greek letters on his mummy. This shows that, like most of the people in the portraits, he was part of the Greek cultured elite, almost certainly with Greek ancestry. His features seem to reflect his status – a long, noble face with a prominent nose and a strong mouth. On his thick dark hair he wears a gold wreath, perhaps a sign of nobility. Yet the fact he was mummified at all indicates that he and his family had adopted Egyptian funerary practices. The mummy case is covered with Egyptian deities and symbols connected with death and rebirth (see overleaf).

Two mummies were found with him and were decorated so similarly that it can be assumed that they were probably relatives. One was also called Artemidorus and may have been his father; while the other, a woman (possibly his mother), was called Thermoutharin, a very Egyptian-sounding name. This cultural fusion is further enriched by his very Roman-style portrait, on which, it was planned, his family and his descendants could gaze for generations to come.

Artemidorus was discovered on 3 April 1888, the day that Hawara was visited by Heinrich Schliemann, the famous excavator of Troy. Petrie describes a day of a 'concentration of pleasures which if properly beaten out would have sufficed to gild a fortnight'. Schliemann witnessed a 'procession of three gilt mummies … coming across the mounds, glittering in the sun. These are of a fresh style, three painted portraits, but the body covered with a bright red-brown varnish and scenes in relief gilt all over it. The name on each mummy across the breast. These I must bring away intact, they are so fine and in such good condition.'

PORTRAIT OF A WOMAN
Hawara, AD 100–120

An elaborate hairstyle with banks of curls frames this woman's perfectly round face. A long plait coiled into an imposing bun sits on the crown of her head, her cheeks are full, her lips small and pursed, and her chin fleshy. She wears a complete set of jewellery – a large gold pin to hold her hairstyle in place, a pair of hoop earrings threaded with pearls and emeralds, and two necklaces of gold and emeralds with a large round emerald pendant.

Compared to the other female portraits, this woman's face appears fuller and fleshier, but in Greek and Roman society this was considered an indication of physical (and financial) well-being. Interestingly, Petrie tells us she was found on Valentine's Day (14 February) 1888: 'Just before sunset a boy came up announcing another mummy ... a good one in perfect preservation of a youngish lady wearing 2 necklaces.'

PORTRAIT OF A WOMAN
Hawara, *c.* AD 100–120

This portrait of a rather frail young woman is one of the most graceful, delicate and best-preserved ever found at Hawara. Her hairstyle, with its thick curls and short ringlets in front of the ears, dates her to the early second century AD. She wears gold and emerald hoop earrings and two necklaces, one that matches her earrings and another with gold, amethysts and a central emerald with pendant pearls. Her elegant light-purple (cyclamen) robes are amongst the most skilfully painted and beautifully coloured from Hawara. Her diaphanous purple scarf is draped decorously over her shoulders, and under this her tunic can be seen clearly falling off her right shoulder. This may be a conscious imitation of the way that the goddess of love and desire Aphrodite/Venus was sometimes portrayed. Petrie described the portrait as 'a charming head of a girl, with an ingenuous sparkling expression, yet very modern in appearance, such as one might meet in any drawing room nowadays'.

PORTRAIT OF A WOMAN
Hawara, AD 120–140

This young woman lived in the city of Arsinoe between about AD 120 and 140, during the period that the emperor Hadrian ruled the Roman empire. We can tell this from her hairstyle which, with its curled front and large coiled bun, is typical of portraiture of ladies of the imperial court at the time. Her robes are coloured a delicate light purple and she wears fine jewellery including a pair of gold and pearl hoop earrings and two necklaces with pearls, emeralds and garnets. But her face has disproportionately large eyes and a rather mechanically drawn nose and mouth, which give her a rather lifeless feel. Unusually the portrait is still squared and has not been cut down into the arched or angular shape used for insertion into the mummy. Nevertheless, we know from Petrie's records that this portrait was indeed found over the head of a mummy; the two dark strips of resin at the long sides of the portrait also indicate that it was actually used.

PORTRAIT OF A MAN
Hawara, *c.* AD 140–160

This middle-aged man fixes us with an intense, authoritative gaze. His features, though rendered rather impressionistically, convey a sense of quiet and inner strength. He has a long straight nose, a fairly small mouth and thick curly hair with a full beard and moustache suggesting a date in the middle of the second century AD. In his hair he wears a band with a central seven-pointed star, almost certainly a religious symbol, and three short locks of hair fan out from under the star. The hairstyle and the star may indicate that he was involved in the worship of the god Serapis, a fusion of Greek and Egyptian gods who became one of Egypt's most important deities in the Roman period.

Petrie was particularly pleased with this portrait. It was one of the last to be discovered in his 1911 excavations, but was clearly by no means the least. Petrie described it as 'one of the finest, a middle-aged man of Homeric type, with a … seven pointed star on his hair, … probably a badge of some office or priesthood. It is of splendid work and perfect state.'

PORTRAIT OF A YOUNG MAN
Hawara, AD 150–170

An arch of gilded plaster (stucco), finely decorated with vine leaves and grapes, frames this young man's portrait. His light brown eyes and his full but down-turned mouth give an impression of world-weariness or sadness. His thick dark hair, moustache and beard probably place him in the middle of the second century AD, the time of the 'philosopher' emperor Marcus Aurelius.

In technique, the painting is less well executed than some, with shade and tone provided by means of quite heavy diagonal strokes, yet it is framed so beautifully. We are not sure of the significance of such frames, but they are quite rare, and they may indicate that the person was of very high status. On the other hand they may simply show that the family paid a little more for 'extras' at the time of mummification. The portrait has certainly been treated with considerable respect, with only a small area of the robes discoloured by the mummification bandages.

This was Petrie's twenty-fifth portrait, excavated on 29 February 1888: 'a youngish man ... of good ordinary style and in very good state ... a border of gilt stucco with vine in relief all around.'

PORTRAIT OF A WOMAN
Hawara, AD 160–180

This lady is perhaps one of the most refined of the Hawara portraits. Her complexion is so smooth and her expression so serene that she could have stepped out of a dinner party in Edwardian England. Her hair is neatly arranged and she wears a pair of gold earrings with large pearls, and two necklaces, one of emeralds and the other of gold. Her features are finely drawn, with high cheekbones, a long well-defined nose and full lips. Her graceful air is spoilt only by the dark stain that covers most of her right eye and eyebrow. Interestingly someone has made a very haphazard repair, including the use of red paint in an attempt to redefine the damaged eye. The effect is far from satisfactory, and some have suggested (wrongly) that the restoration was carried out by the excavator Petrie himself. Instead, it is almost certain that the area was treated in antiquity in order to correct problems of oil staining which had occurred during the mummification process.

Petrie records the discovery of the portrait on 7 March 1888: 'the digger ... bearing the mamma with a good panel portrait – unluckily part of the forehead and one eye damaged by oil run from the brat above.' The 'brat' was a 'small child with painted panel portrait, of good work, in perfect condition' found directly above her, and was very possibly her daughter. The little girl is now in the Cairo Museum, Egypt, one of a dozen or so portraits that Grebaut, the Director of the museum, selected from Petrie's 1888 finds.

PORTRAIT OF A WOMAN
Hawara, *c.* AD 190–220?

This woman, with her wild frizzy hairstyle and enigmatic elfin smile, stands out from the other female portraits. Although the surface is quite badly damaged, it is still possible to make out her (over) large eyes, fine nose and broad smiling mouth. The unusual proportions of her eyes and the rough brushstrokes of her face and neck might suggest the painter's skill wasn't equal to his enthusiasm. Putting a date to the painting is quite difficult. In any other portrait, her short curled hairstyle would suggest she lived in the later second century AD, but her jewellery includes a crescent pendant that belongs to the first century. If she did live in that earlier period, then her hair does not really fit into the main fashions of the empire. In that case, this may be an example of a native Egyptian or North African hairstyle – an unusual feature in the portraits.

PORTRAIT OF A WOMAN
Hawara, *c.* AD 190–220

If this rather ghostly portrait had not been so badly damaged it would be considered one of the most elaborate and interesting of the group. A woman is shown festooned with jewellery, all picked out in gold leaf. On her head is a gilded wreath with triangular and diamond-shaped elements, and a central disk. She wears a pair of trident earrings with pearl terminals, and two gold necklaces with bars and chevron elements and a gemstone pendant. Even her lips are gilded – a very rare feature in mummy portraits.

In contrast to most portraits in which the subject is painted slightly at an angle to the viewer, this woman is shown facing completely forwards. The panel is also unusual in that it has a black border around the upper edge and the sides. This indicates that, like the portrait on p. 46, it is complete and has not been cut down from a larger panel. The portrait must originally have been very striking, but the damage to the eye and other parts of the face is quite severe. As Petrie said of this portrait and others discovered in January 1911: 'More portraits coming in, but nearly all much damaged with oil from the mummies.'

PORTRAIT OF A WOMAN
Hawara, *c.* AD 50–70

This is a remarkable portrait because it was found in a wooden frame, making it the only true, framed 'picture' to survive from Hawara. The frame is well preserved, but the portrait is very badly damaged. Much of the original paint, particularly on the body and the right side of the face, is missing or has flaked and been displaced on the surface. From what remains, we can identify the subject as a dark-haired woman wearing traces of a necklace and pearl earrings.

The frame is made of double-grooved pieces of wood, which, Petrie suggested, 'gives us an excellent pattern for glazing'. Illustrated examples of this 'Oxford' type of frame are found as far afield as Kertch in the Ukraine and Leicester in England. The original palm-tree fibre cord for suspending the painting is still attached to the corners of the frame.

This portrait is much smaller than the others featured in this book and could not properly have covered the face of a mummy. In fact, it was not found over a head at all, but rather propped against the legs of a mummy that apparently had never had a portrait. Petrie suggested that it was 'painted to be kept in the house for years until the survivors had had enough of it'.

PORTRAITS FROM ER-RUBAYAT

PORTRAIT OF A WOMAN
Er-Rubayat, *c.* AD 100–120

The cheerful character of this woman shines through the rather amateurish painting of the portrait. Her face is oval with eyes that are far too large, an impressionistic nose and a smiling mouth that is typical of er-Rubayat portraits – fleshy and bow-shaped. She is covered in jewellery, including a pair of trident earrings with pearl terminals, a snake bracelet and a triple-banded ring. She also wears two necklaces, one with gold and emeralds and the other with gold chevron motifs and a crescent pendant.

In her hand she holds a small *unguentarium,* or bottle for scented oils, which were often placed in graves as offerings to the dead. Here, perhaps, it is simply intended to represent a bottle of her favourite perfume. Her hair is a mass of dense curls with tight ringlets falling over her brow and by her ears; it may even be a wig. Wigs were popular in the Roman empire and had a long history in Egypt, where several examples have been found in tombs, preserved by the very dry conditions.

PORTRAIT OF AN ELDERLY WOMAN
Er-Rubayat, *c.* AD 100–140

M ost of the other portraits in this book seem to reflect
something of the role and status of their subjects as
the elite of this part of Roman Egypt. However, this lady looks
as though she might have had a very difficult life. Even
allowing for the generally limited skills of the 'er-Rubayat'
painters, it is unusual to see quite such a harsh treatment of a
subject. The over-long nose, huge uneven eyes and unrealistic
mouth are all typical of this group, but this poor woman has
much more. Her hair, assuming she does not have a bun at
the back of her head, is cropped short and is shot through
dramatically with grey. Implausibly straight (and deep)
wrinkles furrow her brow, and there are heavy lines indicative
of age (and perhaps exposure to the sun) under her eyes,
around her mouth and on her neck.

Unique among the female portraits, she wears no jewellery
at all. The headband is the only possible 'adornment', though
this was probably functional. Her appearance certainly
suggests someone who has worked hard all her life, possibly
manually. Yet, either she or someone else paid to have her
portrait painted and her body mummified, perhaps by setting
aside a portion of their small income. It is conceivable that
she was a valued servant or slave, in which case her owners
may have provided for her funeral and burial, complete with
portrait.

PORTRAIT OF A YOUNG MAN
Er-Rubayat, *c.* AD 110–130

This young man has several of the features that characterize the er-Rubayat portraits – the over-large eyes, the fleshy, slightly smiling lips and the sketchily drawn hair and clothing. But the eyes, though far too big for the portrait, are painted with a certain skill, and combined with the half-smiling mouth create a rather arresting expression.

His hair is brought forward and cut quite short, suggesting he probably lived at the time of the emperor Trajan in the early second century. His wispy moustache and beard indicate that he was probably only in his early twenties, the typical age of many of the subjects of these portraits, reflecting the low life expectancy of the time.

PORTRAIT OF A MAN
Er-Rubayat, *c.* AD 120–140

This bearded man, shown in his late twenties or thirties, has the typically over-large eyes, pillar-nose and thick lips of er-Rubayat portraits. His mouth is extremely fleshy and pursed, contrasting with the much more realistic masculine facial hair. In fact, if you only saw his eyes, nose and mouth you would not know whether it was a man or a woman, so uniform are the features in these portraits. His thick beard, moustache and rather unruly, curly hair date him to the Hadrianic era, around AD 120–140. Hadrian was the first emperor to have a beard, which, up until then, had been primarily a Greek fashion. Further evidence that er-Rubayat portraits were sometimes painted by unskilled artists can be seen in the shoulder stripes (*clavi*) of his tunic, which continue right over the scarf on his shoulders (just visible here).

PORTRAIT OF A WOMAN
Er-Rubayat, *c.* AD 160–170

This stunning young woman is perhaps one of the most beautiful portraits to have survived from Roman Egypt. In every way she is exceptional. Her hair is short but very elegantly dressed, with a series of tight waves framing her forehead. This style was very popular amongst wealthy Roman women in the AD 160s–170s, but she could also quite easily have stepped out of 1930s Europe, with a fashionable 'Marcel wave' perm. She has very fine facial features, in particular her carefully modelled eyes and her finely proportioned mouth, adding to her air of wealth and high status. The play of light on her face and neck is very expertly realized. Her drapery (see overleaf) is quite unusual: her shoulder stripe (*clavus*), shown in gold, joins up with a gold border around the neck opening of her tunic; this is something not seen on any other portrait. In addition, her scarf, instead of falling over her left shoulder, is drawn right across her chest. Her jewellery is also very striking. She wears emerald earrings with large drop pearls and a very ostentatious necklace of gold set with emeralds, a great central garnet, and (possibly worked) lozenges of gold. In her hair she wears a wreath made of fine gold leaf, and gold leaf is also used to pick out the details of her jewellery and even for the edges of the gold decoration of her robes.

But behind this extraordinary portrait there is a detective story. Every aspect is so well executed that it towers above most of the other er-Rubayat examples. The fine attention to facial

details and the quality of the clothing and jewellery point to
Hawara rather than er-Rubayat; so, too, does the arched shape
of the portrait and the fact that it was painted on a thin
veneer of wood rather than the heavy boards that are typical
of er-Rubayat. Even the technique used to paint it – the
'encaustic' technique, in which pigments were mixed with
melted wax – was largely alien to er-Rubayat, but by far the
most common method at Hawara.

The Hawara portraits illustrate people who lived in the
provincial capital at Arsinoe, while the er-Rubayat examples
were painted for the elite of the smaller city of Philadelphia,
to the north. Is it possible that one of the wealthier families
from Philadelphia commissioned an artist from Arsinoe? Or
was this beautiful woman not from Philadelphia at all?
Er-Rubayat was assumed to be the findspot of this portrait
because it formed part of the collections of Count Theodor
Graf of Vienna, who acquired most of the portraits associated
with this site. Petrie's journals, however, may suggest a further
explanation. He laments that while he was temporarily absent
from Hawara in 1888 'old Faraq, the Arab dealer was allowed
to work at Hawara ... but he only got 4 or 5 portraits'. Could
this then be a member of a refined family from Arsinoe,
whose portrait was excavated and spirited away while Petrie's
back was turned?

PORTRAIT OF A MILITARY OFFICER
Er-Rubayat, *c.* AD 160–170

The realistic face of a man stares out from a rather dark portrait. His eyes are small but full of life, his nose is well drawn and his mouth is upturned in a knowing smile. His eyebrows, moustache and beard are full and thick, while his hair is a mass of dark tousled curls. He was probably in his late twenties when he died, and he looks very similar to portraits of the emperor Lucius Verus, who reigned in the AD 160s. The quality of the painting is exceptional for er-Rubayat, and it is possible that, like the previous portrait, this one may originally have been found at Hawara, the cemetery of Arsinoe, the capital of this part of Egypt. Alternatively the man's family may have been wealthy enough to have commissioned the portrait from an artist from Arsinoe or another centre.

But wherever he was from, and wherever he was buried, this man was no ordinary citizen. His clothing and accessories show that he was an officer in the Roman army. Over his left shoulder he wears a *sagum* (military cloak), fastened at his shoulder by a gold bow-shaped fibula (brooch). Under the *sagum* and across his chest is a red leather *balteus* (sword belt) decorated with gold discs. Was he an Egyptian who had fought for Rome and was buried in his native land, or did he die during a posting far away from home? Probably, he was a local man – he was, after all, mummified, though the allure of Egypt's culture and customs for the foreigners who settled there should not be underestimated.

PORTRAIT OF A WOMAN
Er-Rubayat, *c.* AD 160–180

Here is one of the most impressionistic portraits to have survived. As we can see by comparing average portraits from Hawara and er-Rubayat, there is a noticeable difference in quality between the two places. Yet, even by the variable standards of the er-Rubayat artists, this lady is extremely naively painted.

Her hair is simply piled up in sketchily drawn curls, above a worryingly high forehead. Her eyes are without pupils and are unusually wide. Her nose and mouth are painted in the amateurish style so typical of er-Rubayat. Her jewellery makes the only link with historical reality – a pair of gold hoop earrings and two necklaces, which date her to the later second century.

The very poor standard of painting might suggest a different intended use for the Hawara and er-Rubayat portraits. Those from Hawara were almost certainly kept in tomb temples for several generations. As Petrie commented: 'I had suspected that the mummies – especially those with portraits – were kept above ground … for perhaps years and then finally interred.' In contrast, perhaps the purpose of many of the er-Rubayat portraits was simply to decorate the mummy during the final ceremonies of burial.

PORTRAIT OF A WOMAN
Er-Rubayat, *c.* AD 190–210

T his rather severe lady looks beyond us, into the distance.
Her broad angular face has irregularly spaced eyes, a long
pinched nose and a wide, fleshy bow mouth. The roughly
sketched hair is curled tightly to her head and dates her to the
later second century AD. Her jewellery also belongs to that
period. She wears a pair of gold trident earrings with pearl
terminals, and a gold chain with a round pendant bearing the
face of Medusa (see p. 80).

PORTRAIT OF A WOMAN
Er-Rubayat, *c.* AD 190–210

This young woman looks quite pensive, as though she has been distracted by something in the distance. Her face is quite well proportioned by the standards of the er-Rubayat portraits, and her features are competently drawn (even if her eyes, eerily, have no pupils). Her hair is massed on either side of a central parting, and individual curls are drawn over the top of the hair and around her brow, a style that was popular in the later second century AD. Her clothes seem traditional – she wears a tunic with a scarf over her left shoulder – but there is a third garment, indicated by a white fringe (of tassels perhaps) that runs along her shoulders.

Most of her jewellery – a pair of pearl hoop earrings and a necklace of gold and sapphires – is typical of that worn by women all over the empire. But the gold chain with a circular pendant that almost certainly bore the face of the Gorgon Medusa is a more local item (see p. 80). These pendants are shown on mummy portraits of the second century, nearly always from er-Rubayat. This might suggest that they were a fashion of that particular period and possibly that particular region.

GOLD MEDUSA NECKLACE
Second century AD

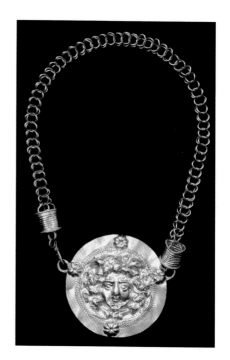

Several of the women shown in the er-Rubayat portraits wear necklaces like this one. It is called a Medusa necklace because the central medallion bears the face of the Gorgon Medusa. In Greek mythology the Gorgons were three snake-haired she-demons, with the power to turn anyone who looked at them to stone. Medusa, the queen of the Gorgons, was killed by the Greek hero Perseus. He did not look at her directly, but cleverly watched her reflection in the shield that the goddess Athena had given him. He cut off Medusa's head and gave it to Athena, who put it on the centre of her shield. The Gorgon's head (*gorgoneion*), with its characteristic snake-hair, was adopted by the Greeks and Romans as an apotropaic symbol, to ward off evil and bring good fortune. It was used on buildings, shields and breast-plates and was very popular, as here, on jewellery.

PORTRAITS FROM OTHER SITES

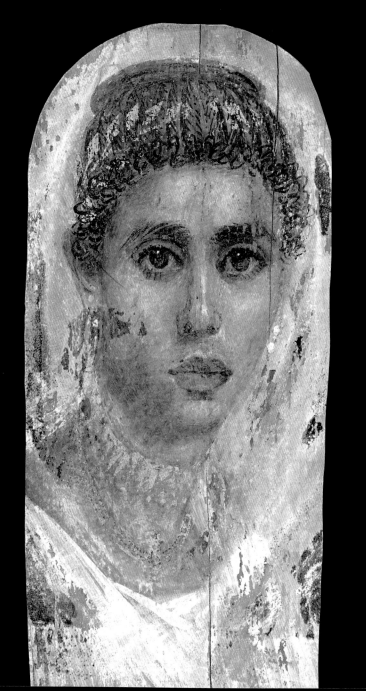

PORTRAIT OF A WOMAN
Saqqara, c. AD 100–120

The discovery of mummy portraits is not just confined to the Fayum area; sites all over Egypt have produced examples. This beautiful young woman with her rich jewellery was found at Saqqara, the cemetery of the important city of Memphis, in the north of Egypt.

Everything about her portrait is striking, in particular her very well-defined features. Her brown eyes with their thick brows are remarkably realistic. She has high cheekbones, a small well-formed nose and very full lips. Her dark complexion is effectively rendered through subtle shades and highlights. Her hair is tightly plaited and drawn back into segments – the so-called 'melon' hairstyle. This is very similar to modern 'cornrows', inspired by African hairstyles. At the top of her head is a large coiled bun, and there is a series of curls framing the brow. Her face and her hairstyle make it very likely that she had some North African or sub-Saharan ancestry.

Her jewellery is mostly picked out in gold leaf – a necklace of long, triangular segments with bead terminals and a heavy chain with a central pendant. The pendant is in the form of an *ankh* – the Egyptian symbol of life. But her earrings are typically Roman hoops of pearls, reflecting the cultural mix of the empire.

FRAGMENTARY PORTRAIT OF A WOMAN
Possibly Memphis, *c.* AD 140–160

This vertical fragment preserves part of the face of a woman, who peers at us, as if though a door left ajar or a shuttered window. Enough survives to show that she had finely waved hair (dating her to the middle of the second century AD) and wore jewellery, including a large gold hairpin, pearl earrings and a gold rope-style necklace.

Even though she is incomplete, the lady has an interesting history. She was probably excavated in the 1820s at Memphis, one of the most important cities in the north of Egypt. Her excavator, Count Louis de Laborde, was a French aristocrat, who kept the portrait in his private collection. The piece was later sold to Louis Philippe I of France. It came to the British Museum through the sale of the king's estate and was one of the earliest portraits to enter the museum collections.

FRAGMENTARY PORTRAIT
OF A WOMAN
Provenance unknown, *c.* AD 100–120

This tantalizing sliver of wood preserves a small part of a young woman's face. Her fine nose is well preserved, and we can also make out the bottom of her right eye (she seems to be looking to the side) and much of her right ear. In front of her ear are tight ringlets, and hanging below them is a gold hoop earring threaded with pearls. Enough remains to date her to around AD 100. By the side of her face is part of her name, 'Sarapi(as)', written in Greek letters, which indicates that she almost certainly had Greek ancestors. However, the name itself is linked to Sarapis – the main Egyptian deity in Greek and Roman times. Named portraits are very rare, and it is a shame that this example is so fragmentary. But even so, her name is still spoken, she is still remembered and so her memory lives on, just as she and her family would have wished.

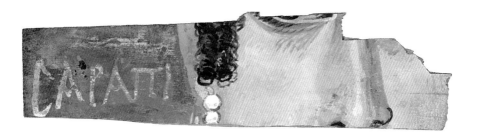

FULL-LENGTH PORTRAIT
OF A YOUTH
Thebes, *c.* AD 200–250

This young man still smiles out from the brightly painted shroud that wrapped his mummy. Details of his clothes, in particular the folded scarf around his shoulders and over his chest, indicate he lived in the early to mid-third century AD. In his hands he holds a pink garland and sprigs of the sacred plant myrtle. His lower body is covered by an apron, decorated with a criss-cross design and a winged sun-disc.

The mummy was found at Thebes, the ancient capital of Egypt. Outside the city, in the Valley of the Kings, were the tombs of some of Egypt's most famous pharaohs, including Ramesses II and Tutankhamun. The city remained prosperous during the Greek and Roman periods and its monumental temples such as Karnak and Luxor can still be seen. It is interesting to think that he saw them complete and in their full glory.

PORTRAIT OF A WOMAN ON
A PAINTED SHROUD
Provenance unknown, *c.* AD 190–220

This is another example of a portrait painted on a linen shroud, a fashion typical in the later second and early third centuries AD. The woman looks at us face on, and holds out a cup of wine as if asking us to toast her departure to the afterlife. She is dressed in her finest clothes – a white undertunic and a rose-pink tunic with a matching broad scarf, brought down from her shoulders and draped over her lower body. On the scarf is a prominent right-angled motif – a stylized version of the Greek letter 'gamma', which was used decoratively on fine clothing in the Roman empire.

Her features are small and soft, and in her left hand is a folded garland of flowers. The overall impression is one of a calm and gentle transition to the next life. She stands in a gilded frame with painted emeralds and other precious stones, and is surrounded by scenes of Egyptian deities including two women with vulture wings who spread their wings around her head to protect her during her journey.

PORTRAIT OF A YOUTH SET INTO A MUMMY
Provenance unknown, *c.* AD 140–180

W ith his big eyes and bright smile. this young man's portrait is very arresting. However, when you look more closely, you can see that the eyes are actually a little too big and the mouth is a rather strange shape. His hairstyle suggests he lived in the second century AD and a CAT scan of his body indicates he died in late adolescence.

His mummy was bandaged in the normal way and was then wrapped in a plain sheet of linen, which bound the portrait onto the mummy's head. At some stage after its discovery, the portrait was taken off the mummy, damaging the linen and exposing the criss-crossed bandages. It has now been reattached and the boy's mummy is complete again.

FULL-LENGTH PORTRAIT
OF A BOY
Provenance unknown, *c.* AD 230–250

T his little boy is wrapped in his
original shroud and still lies in
his traditionally Egyptian wooden
coffin. The shroud is painted with a
full-length picture of the child, who
looks to be about ten years old;
recent CAT scans of his body have
confirmed this. The shroud itself is
very well preserved and has a
patterned border of intertwined
ribbons and leaves.

He looks at us with his big brown
eyes, his age emphasized by his
shaved head with four locks of hair, a
style typical for young boys. He wears
a red garland on his head and holds
twigs of myrtle in his left hand. Myrtle
was a sacred plant and sprigs and
wands of it were found by Petrie in
several tombs at Hawara. Details of the
boy's drapery suggest he may have been
painted in about AD 230–250, making
him one of the latest of the mummy
portraits.

CHRONOLOGY

Dates of key Roman emperors coinciding
with the period of the portraits

Claudius AD 41–54

Nero AD 54–68

Vespasian AD 69–79

Titus AD 79–81

Domitian AD 81–96

Nerva AD 96–98

Trajan AD 98–117

Hadrian AD 117–138

Antoninus Pius AD 138–161

Marcus Aurelius AD 161–180 / Lucius Verus AD 161–169

Commodus AD 180–192

Septimius Severus AD 193–211

Caracalla AD 211–217

Elagabalus AD 217–222

Alexander Severus AD 222–235

FURTHER READING

W.M.F. Petrie 1889, *Hawara, Biahmu and Arsinoe*. London

W.M.F. Petrie 1890, *Kahun, Gurob and Hawara*. London

W.M.F. Petrie 1911, *Roman Portraits and Memphis* (IV). London

W.M.F. Petrie 1913, *The Hawara Portfolio: Portraits of the Roman Age*. London

W.M.F. Petrie 1931, *Seventy Years in Archaeology*. London

M.S. Drower 1985, *Flinders Petrie – A Life in Archaeology*. London

K. Parlasca, *Ritratti di Mummie, Repertorio d'Arte dell'Egitto Greco Romano* (four vols). 1969, 1977, 1980 Palermo; 2003 Rome

E. Doxiadis 1995, *The Mysterious Fayum Portraits: Faces from Ancient Egypt*. London

S.E.C. Walker and M.L. Bierbrier 1997, *Ancient Faces: Mummy Portraits from Roman Egypt*. London

M.L. Bierbrier (ed.) 1997, *Portraits and Masks: Burial Customs in Roman Egypt*. London

J. Picton, S. Quirke and P. Roberts 2007, *Living Images: Egyptian Funerary Portraits in the Petrie Museum*. Walnut Creek

ILLUSTRATION REFERENCES

All illustrations © The Trustees of
the British Museum, except for p.9
(Paul Roberts).

The British Museum registration
numbers for the mummy portraits
illustrated:

p.2 EA 74716
pp.14/15 EA 21809
p.16 EA 74719
p.18 EA 74709
p.20 EA 74716
pp.22/5 EA 74713
p.26 EA 74707
p.28 EA 74718
p.30 EA 74711
p.32 EA 74715
p.34 EA 74708
p.37 EA 13595
pp.38/40 EA 21810
p.42 EA 74712
pp.44/5 EA 74706
p.46 EA 74705

p.48 EA 74714
p.50 EA 74704
p.52 EA 74710
p.54 EA 74703
p.56 EA 74717
p.58 GRA 1889.10–18.1
p.60 EA 63395
p.62 GRA 1890.9–20.1
p.64 EA 63397
p.66 EA 63396
pp.68/71 EA 65346
p.72 EA 65345
p.74 EA 63394
p.76 EA 65344
p.78 EA 65343
p.80 GRA 1917.6–1.2737
p.82 EA 29772
p.84 EA 5619
p.85 GRA 1890.8–1.2
pp.86/7 EA 6709
p.88 EA 68509
pp.90/1 EA 6713
pp.92/3 EA 6715